I0543041

Travis I. Sivart

27 Thoughts on Life Omnibus

Travis I. Sivart

Travis I. Sivart

27 Thoughts on Life Omnibus
27 Thoughts on Life Series

ISBN: 1519454813
ISBN-13: 9781519454812

Talk of the Tavern Publishing Group

27 Thoughts on Life Omnibus

Introduction

Hello, and I'm so thrilled that you picked up this book. The technicals of this work is that it's four books put together. This volume contains 27 Thoughts on Enjoying Life, 27 Thoughts on Having No Regrets in Life, 27 Thoughts on Phrases That Changed My Life, and 27 Thoughts on Profound Sayings. I've brought them together and kept the price as low as possible. These books aren't about making money, they're about helping people. Share them with others, give copies to someone who needs to hear the things within these covers, and let others know your thoughts by leaving a review.

I wrote the first in 2015 for deeply personal reasons, and continued with the others until 2019. They are all meaningful to me, and the sort of knowledge I hope to pass down to my children and young people who I care about.

There is a foreword for each volume which explains more about that particular book, and each is available individually, but I felt this book needed to be in the world.

Thank you for reading, and I hope all the hope for you and yours.

~ Travis I. Sivart

Travis I. Sivart

Contents

Travis I. Sivart

27 Thoughts on Enjoying Life

Travis I. Sivart

Dedication

To those that have helped me by listening, and also by talking. But mostly to all those I love, have loved, and will love that fight this battle each and every day, a battle that most people cannot see or imagine.

27 Thoughts on Life Omnibus

Acknowledgements

I want to thank all the great teachers that have influenced my life. Since my childhood forward I have had an ensemble cast of eclectic characters showing me how to roll with the punches, and when to stop taking a hit. From friends and family, to granola crunching bestselling authors, to scientific research, they have all helped me grow.

Thanks to Lee, Kat, Emma, Elizabeth, Richard, Angela, Tami, Markell, Chris, Kyle, Deborah, and all the others who gave input about their personal experiences with depression. A special thank you to Jody Neil Ruth for his blog and short movie, Demons.

Travis I. Sivart

Foreword

I have a good life and am usually happy, and I wanted to give something back. This book is a collection of suggestions which I have learned throughout my life that guide me and help me stay happy. Nothing here is new or revolutionary, and many self-help or "how to be successful" books offer similar suggestions. I especially wanted to reach out to people who face the daily challenge of depression.

Winston Churchill called depression the big "black dog" and fought with it throughout his life. He didn't claim to have beaten it, rather to have tamed it. I don't know if he specifically meant the following about depression, but he offered this advice, "Never give in, never give in, never, never, never, in nothing, great or small, large or petty — never give in…" It is great advice, and by never giving up you guarantee you will never fail.

I am not a mental health professional, though I have had some schooling in psychology. I am just some guy who listens a lot, asks a few questions, and listens some more. Many people have suggested I should be a therapist, but I have never felt that would be a good fit for me because I am too blunt and honest for most people seeking therapy.

I have never battled depression, unless you count having a "down" day or two. I have thoughts of my demise, usually a couple times a year. But those thoughts don't last even a whole minute before I move on from them, replacing them with more constructive thoughts. Though I am generally upbeat, sometimes I do have an "escape" day where I hide under blankets, sip a scotch, and watch movies until I am too tired to stay awake.

I have lost more than one friend to suicide from depression. I have watched my own mother battle depression and alcoholism, and never quite get out from under them. I have had friends that I had known for over twenty years, who always seemed happy and at the top of their game to the outside world, end it all. As I write this, I am worried about two more friends that I have known for decades who are battling depression and possible suicide. I don't know if it is normal to know so many folks who fight with this, or if depression is a common challenge, (if it is, we need a lot more attention on it) or if I am a special person to whom folks open up to with their problems. I do know I have kept more friends that battled this affliction than I have lost. So far.

I tell you all this so you know a little bit about who I am. I can understand the mindset of depression, perhaps even relate, but at minimum I can empathize. If you don't think I have the background, formal education, or right to talk about this since I have not battled with it personally… just put this book down and walk away. If you have already judged me, nothing I say beyond this point will change your mind.

While writing this I consulted with many friends who battle depression, asking for their input and what techniques they use to manage their condition on a daily basis.

I did not write this to make money; I will always have this available for free to anyone who wants it. I didn't write this to get attention for myself. I simply write this from decades of experience of helping those close to me. I say helping because, and I will reiterate this many times, I can't fix anyone's problems or fight the fight for them. I am only a coach, and you have put on the gloves and step into the ring. I will be here to give you advice, check your wounds, and wipe the sweat from your eyes, but you have to do the hard part. You have to fight this fight, and fight to win. You can never let your guard down or take a rest while in the ring, or you will get knocked down… and each time you get knocked to the mat, it is a bit harder to get up. So, let's get you the training you need to go the distance, and not get knocked down.

This book is not meant for those on the edge of a cliff, literally or figuratively, and preparing to commit suicide. If you are in that place, call someone. Now. Anyone. I will give some helpful suggestions after the foreword. This is the preventative and maintenance guide, not a one-stop fix-it shop.

No one thing will fix it. Faith, friends, medicine, and everything else are viable tools. They are all good things when used correctly. Find what works for you, but it is a combination of tools that will work best. Mental wellness is a journey, not a destination. It all starts and ends with you doing the work. Those other things can help, but you have to be an active participant. No one can do the hard part for you.

A note on medicine, get it if you need it. Don't feel bad if you need it, it is a tool to help. Talk to more than one doctor, research the medicines, and pay close attention to what changes with each modification in your meds type or dosage. Take an active part in what you are prescribed, you may not be a doctor, but it is your body and you should know it better than anyone else.

~Travis I. Sivart

Helpful links and sites for depression and/or suicide:

UK:
www.mind.org.uk
www.samaritans.org

USA:
www.agoracares.org
www.suicidepreventionlifeline.org
www.thesemicolonproject.com
www.yourlifeyourvoice.org
memphiscrisiscenter.org

International:
www.supportisp.org

1. Forgive Yourself

No one is perfect and we are all allowed to have bad days and make mistakes. You're no different. Forgive yourself and move on. Don't dwell on things that cause you to doubt or even hate yourself.

Allow yourself mistakes and bad days. You are not wrong or weak for feeling the way you feel, and many more people than you realize deal with these same issues. It is ok to not always be at your best, and you have to let yourself experience the full spectrum of life, feelings, emotions, triumphs, and failures. That is how we live and grow. But learn to let go of the bad stuff, don't let it drag you down.

Travis I. Sivart

2. Know Someone Cares

It is hard to see at times, but people do care. Sometimes it is the people around you, other times it is a complete stranger. But people do care about you and what happens to you.

Believe the people who tell you that they care. Allow yourself to be liked, cared for, worried about, or even loved. And also believe you deserve it and are worth caring about.

Travis I. Sivart

3. Baby Steps

Nothing happens instantly. Everything takes time. Especially when it comes to getting your life and your head straight. Some days it comes easy, other days it feels like it is a million miles away. That's ok.

Take baby steps. Little by little is a good pace. Let yourself build slowly and realize that every step is progress.

Travis I. Sivart

4. Laugh. Often, Openly, & Honestly

Many people would argue that laughter is healing, and some even say it is the best medicine. Now, I don't think there is any scientific proof of that, but I do know it makes you feel better. Allow yourself to laugh whenever you can. And not just ironic or sarcastic laughter, but good, full, rich, belly laughs if you can manage it.

Watch movies that make you laugh, watch stand-up comedy, YouTube videos of kittens frolicking, or whatever makes you smile then giggle, titter, and guffaw.

Travis I. Sivart

5. Shut down Mental Movies

We all have those mental movies. Some call them daydreams. Perhaps it is while you're standing in a line and someone cuts in front of us, you imagine how it could play out – from ignoring them to a witty put down, to a fist fight. It could be wondering if there will be confrontation when you get to work or home. Whatever it is, if it creates anxiety in you, learn to stop that mental movie. They aren't healthy and only lead to bad places.

Be a director for your head films and actively participate. If you can't shut them down – and most of us can't - try adding cream pies to them. Or squirrels, dinosaurs, famous cartoon characters, or whatever. Just change them enough that they are entertaining instead of trauma inducing.

Travis I. Sivart

6. Be There for Others

Helping other feels good. It gives us a happy rush knowing we did something for others. It gives us a sense of accomplishment and self-worth. Make it a habit to do this every day.

Say good morning to a stranger. Do something nice for them like open a door. Tell a coworker you like their coffee mug or shoes. Compliment people when you can (and it's appropriate) and let them know they are appreciated. You will make their day, and that can make yours.

Listen to others. I mean really listen, don't just wait your turn to talk. You might forget what you were going to say next, but that's ok. Most folks just want to be heard, not to get advice or input; they will let you know if they want more. And your friends always appreciate it when you're there for them. They have you as a friend for a reason, and that reason is because they like you and what you give them in the friendship.

Sometimes the best thing is just knowing you are not alone, and you can show others that others like them are out there by sharing pieces of you, even if it is via social media.

Travis I. Sivart

7. Physical Contact

Human beings are social creatures. Don't overlook the value of accepting physical contact when it is appropriate. A pat on the back, a handshake, or even a hug can help your mood a lot.

With those you are close to, initiate contact. Let your friends and family know that it helps. I am sure they will be willing to show support in that way also, and may need it themselves.

Travis I. Sivart

8. Don't Get Overwhelmed

One thing at a time. One step at a time. Both great rules to live by. Focusing on one thing and completing it gives a sense of accomplishment. It is one key point that any success guide will give, and it applies here also.

Trying too much at once, or even worrying about too much, can make the best of us become overwhelmed and shut down. So take it easy, focus on one task, project, or thing at a time. As long as you are getting something done, then you are making progress. A journey of a thousand miles begins with one step, and it is a lot easier to look for the next place to step than it is to try and look a thousand miles ahead.

Travis I. Sivart

9. Small Achievements

Relating to the previous chapter, small achievements are awesome! Allow yourself to appreciate and even reward yourself for them. If you have to clean your whole house it can be a daunting task. But if you start in one room, it isn't quite as bad. Or start with one task in one room. Maybe it is make the bed, or do the dishes, or pick up anything on the floor. It's easy to do one small task, and when you finish you can go onto the next task.

Appreciate yourself when you have a small achievement. Let yourself feel good, and even reward yourself for it on occasion. The real secret is that a series of small achievements leads to a huge achievement!

Travis I. Sivart

10. Lists

Got a lot to do? Make a list. If it is overwhelming seeing it all on one page, then put each task on a different page. Now break down each task. Cleaning the kitchen is more than one thing. It is dishes, wiping the counter, putting things away, doing the floors, etc. Make each item a part of your list, and check them off. This will let you see that you are making progress and accomplishing things without getting overwhelmed.

Lists also help you remember what is next, because it is often easy to get distracted and wander off. Speaking of which, that is another plus for the list, it helps you focus and keep on task. And when the day is done you have a physical record of your accomplishments!

Travis I. Sivart

11. Celebrate Small Moments

This is kind of like the small achievements I mentioned before, but different. This is not about achievements, but about life. Enjoy and celebrate the small things in life. This is living every candy bar or soda commercial you've ever seen.

Take the time to savor life. Watching a movie with a friend? Make sure to pause and realize how nice it is. Having a delicious snack or meal? Slow down and cherish it. Is the weather nice? Pause and breathe deeply for a few moments. If you can enjoy the small things in life, it makes all the difference.

12. First Things First

To accomplish things it is usually best to start at the beginning of a task. I know that sounds obvious, but many of us will jump right in the middle, and then have to back track. That can make you feel like you got less done because you had to do some things twice. Starting at the beginning allows you to see your whole project come together, whether that is cleaning up your home, writing a book, or putting together a multi-million dollar business deal.

Travis I. Sivart

13. Complain Constructively

We all complain, it is human nature. Some people don't know when to stop though. That can be unhealthy. If you feel the need to complain then make it short, to the point, and make it constructive. Have a purpose, and aim to find a solution. Then you are solving the issue and removing the reason you had to complain, which makes your life less stressful.

Travis I. Sivart

14. Mental Spiral to Chemical Imbalance

Science shows that when we're happy our brain produces certain chemicals. And when we're unhappy, angry, worried, or whatever, our brain produces different chemicals. Some people have the extra challenge in their life of their brains naturally producing extra chemicals of the second type. But the point of this chapter is to not encourage those thoughts that create those chemicals. I know that is easier said than done, but so is everything in this book. This is a daily fight, and it isn't easy, but you can do it.

When feeling that negative spiral coming on it is time to find something else to think about.

15. Do Things for Yourself

You deserve a break today. Take one. Treat yourself to something once in a while. If you can't afford much, then find something you like that you can afford. That might be tasty snack, a good movie, or just an afternoon nap. You deserve rewards for all the hard work you do; let yourself have it.

Treat yourself well. Shower every day, brush your hair and teeth even if you don't have to or don't feel like it, because we feel better when clean. Dress to impress yourself. Don't worry about others. It makes you feel good to look good. And if you feel good about yourself others will notice and be impressed also.

If we can't be good to ourselves, how can we be good for others?

Travis I. Sivart

16. Surround Yourself with Positive People

First and foremost I suggest you surround yourself with others who care and serve your life. I wanted to put this as the first thing in the book, then decided other things should come first, but this is of ultimate importance. The people around you are your support, your example, and your lifeline. Positive and helpful people will help you stay that way also.

Don't keep the negative people in your life. This includes family. Stick with those that are healthy to you. Negative people who are always complaining, using people, or putting others down cause anxiety and stress, which isn't good for you. Don't keep them in your life. If you must deal with them because of a job or whatever, then keep them at arm's length and deal with them only when you need to do so.

Travis I. Sivart

17. Eat Better

I am not going to tell you to diet. I am only going to say to eat better foods. Less processed crap, and keep fast food and junk food to a minimum. Use them as treats if you like, but don't make them a regular diet. Consider a daily multivitamin. Certain vitamins such as vitamin D, B12, B6, and fish oil are said to help our moods. Consult a doctor for more information, and remember too much of anything isn't good.

Healthy food makes you feel better than junk food. The added bonus is that your body processes them better, and since your body is working less to digest, you feel healthier. They make you look better in the long run, and that helps you feel better also. Regular meals help as well, rather than eating at random times.

Travis I. Sivart

18. Eat Smaller Portions

Overeating is a thing we do. Very few people follow the recommended portion sizes. Try it. Eat smaller portions and savor what you're eating. Big heavy meals naturally make us tired and inactive, and that goes hand-in-hand with not getting things done.

Travis I. Sivart

19. Do Something Constructive

Get a hobby. Find something creative and constructive that you enjoy, and do it. Make it something physical so you can see the results. A few examples can be art, knitting, gardening, music, etc. I encourage something that lasts, and though cleaning your house can work in this instance, it doesn't last, which is why I suggest these other things.

So many of us make video games or movies our hobby, but at the end of the day we don't have anything tangible to show for it.

Travis I. Sivart

20. Pay Bills ASAP

Money and bills are a huge stress on our lives. It is a constant worry. Try paying your bills as soon as they come in. It removes that little bit of anxiety and lets you enjoy the day instead. If you can't pay it right now, then don't and put the thought aside. You can worry about it when you get the money.

Travis I. Sivart

21. Keep a Schedule

Keeping a schedule allows you to know when you plan to do things and removes stress. Also our bodies function better when we have a regular sleeping, eating, hygiene, and play schedules. Yes, also schedule in down time and play time, they are important.

Another good thing about a schedule is that you know what to do even on the days you don't feel like doing anything. If you work an odd schedule then plan around it. For example, always shower right when you get up or right after work. Always clean the house the same part of the day, again before or after work. Go grocery shopping on your day off, etc. It is a bit challenging juggling around someone else's schedule (work, kids, whatever) but it can be done.

Travis I. Sivart

22. Exercise

I am not saying you have to join a gym. I simply suggest you do some form of exercise on a regular basis. Take a walk, do pushups, yoga, ride a bike, or whatever. It doesn't have to be an hour long work out either, just ten minutes a day is better than nothing. It doesn't matter what it is, just find something you can do.

The benefits of fitness are physical, of course, but also mental and emotional. It allows you to focus on something and clear your mind.

Travis I. Sivart

23. Stretch

We spend so much time bent over computers, TVs, and so many other things. Hunching has become a way of life. Stretching is healthy and relieves muscle tension. Find a short five or ten minute stretch routine to work out tense and sore muscles. It is good for your whole body, and when your body feels good it helps your mind feel good.

Travis I. Sivart

24. Make an Effort Everyday

Try. That's all. Every day, just try. Put effort into something, even if it is just getting out of bed, showering and getting dressed. Other days you can do more. The days you feel energized will balance out the days you don't. Just make an effort to accomplish something every day. Never give up. The only time you truly fail is if you give up.

Travis I. Sivart

25. Learn to Do Nothing

This is a tough one to learn. Doing nothing is an art the Italians excel at. That is not said snidely either, rather I say it with admiration. It is an art form to do nothing.

Let me define that a little for you. Learn to just sit and relax. No television, no video games, no texting, or whatever. Just relax and enjoy where you are for one hour. Watch the world go by without getting caught in your head or having to have some mundane distraction to keep you preoccupied.

Camping is a great way to do this, but not everyone enjoys or can do that. Try sitting on the front porch, or even just looking out the window. Go to a park and watch the trees, people, and animals. It is truly a gift once you can do this.

Travis I. Sivart

26. Sleep Right

Sleep is one of the most basic needs, and we often don't do it right, or get enough of it. So many of us love to sleep in but have such a hard time getting to sleep when we want or need to. We just can't shut off our head and the thoughts keep coming.

If you have a smart phone or computer you can download an app to help. They play soothing sounds like rain, cats purring, or ocean waves to just mention a few. Counting techniques employed in self-hypnosis often help save my brain from wandering off and keeping me awake with worries. Try different things. And don't worry if they don't work in the first week, keep trying them for a month. If that doesn't work then try another way. Sleep is so important, and so many of us don't do it well. Time to reclaim it.

Travis I. Sivart

27. Now. Right Now.

One of the most important things is being where you are, at this very moment. Many people are constantly worrying about the future or are busy remembering the past. It is ok to plan for the future, but you can't spend all your time wishing it was here already. Same for the past, we can learn from it, we shouldn't forget it, but we can't spend all our time reminiscing about it or regretting what has happened.

Living in the moment means enjoying where you are right now. Appreciating what you have, or who you are with, right at this second. Savoring your current activity or place makes life good. Live what you are doing right now, the past is gone and we can't change it, and the future will be along soon enough. Funny thing is, once we get there, it is now. Live now, right now.

Author's Note

I covered a bit of this in the foreword, but thought I would expand a bit here. The reason I wrote this book was not for me, but for others. For all of my life I have known people who fight depression, and some of them are very good people. They are not weird, or different, not any more than anyone else. They range from kind and giving to self-centered and arrogant. In other words, they are normal.

These are my personal experiences and reasons for me being driven to some small action now. The first person I know of who committed suicide was a friend from elementary school who lived in the neighborhood I grew up in. He was in high school when he did it and we hadn't talked for around six years, so I heard it second hand. I also recall friends in high school who had depression and suicidal thoughts, not that they always go together. I had many friends, (male and female, black and white, gay and straight) call me to talk for hours when they were feeling too down or dangerously self-destructive.

But back in the 80's it wasn't addressed like it is now. We still had the "suck it up" and "tough it out" mentality. But we were headed into a very self-centered decade, the 90's. In the 90's you were allowed to be selfish, whine and cry to get attention, and many did. The ones fighting depression still weren't heard, not really. People thought they were like all the others, especially since people with depression don't tend to cry out much when fighting their demons. Rather, they timidly reach out when they hit a point where they have scared themselves so badly they don't know how to come back without help.

I grew up with an alcoholic mother who went from unhealthy relationship to unhealthy relationship. She went through the classic symptoms of depression, but she wrote them off as anything but that, even blaming it on menopause in the late 80's. I remember begging her to get help, any help at all, and her telling me it was none of my business and sending me away. I remember telling her if it wasn't my business, then I can't keep trying to help. To this day I have no idea if that was the right thing to do, but I do know it shaped our relationship for the rest of our lives.

In my adulthood I continued to have friends call me for help, I guess because I listened. Of course I often tried to "help" by suggesting solutions to their problems, but in time I learned they wanted someone to listen more than they wanted "rescued". And the ones I did "rescue" fell right back into their pattern. I learned that this fight was one they had to do for themselves; I could only support them from the sidelines and let them know I was there when they needed someone.

In 2009 a very close friend who I had known since 1988 killed himself after years of feeling so alone he didn't know what to do. He had not mentioned those feelings to me for over a year, and I thought they had passed until the police came to my door at 1:30 in the morning to give me the news. He had left my name, phone number, and address in his final note as his only friend or family. I still keep his phone number in my cell phone to help remember him.

It is now April 2015 and the year has been an interesting one. As the idea of writing this was brewing in the back of my mind in mid-March, I saw a series of unrelated events, conversations, and coincidences relating to depression and suicide drop at my proverbial doorstep, (including two friends unrelated to each other being hospitalized for self-destructive actions). It solidified my resolve and served as the impetus of dropping everything else and writing this book.

Through the years many friends would call for advice and support. I would often voice the ideas in this book, ideas I use in my life to help me maintain a balance even in the stormiest of times. This whole book is my general life philosophy. I asked many friends who battle depression for their tips and secrets on how they handle their own black dog, and I was happy to hear them echo many of the things in this book. No one mentioned them all, but anything they told me they did was already in this book in one form or another. That reinforcement is what gave me the confidence I needed to put this out there for others.

If this book with its simplistic ideas can help one person in any way, then I am relieved that I published it. Not happy or proud, because this isn't about me. I will just be relieved that someone found something here that helped them.

~Travis I. Sivart

27 Thoughts on Having No Regrets in Life

Travis I. Sivart

Dedication

This book is for my son, friends, and anyone else who listened to me spout ideas and suggestions I have learned.

Introduction

This is a book of advice, ugh. Ever notice the word vice is in advice, just preceded by the suffix of ad? Think about that, and then join me in the next paragraph.

Hey there, glad you made it this far. So, you see my ego in this? Advice is like fish, and opinions are like buttholes; Google that stuff and you'll see. Anyhow, this is stuff I have passed on to my own children, as well as friends – younger and older – when they are seeking counsel. Now, I pass it on in the form of a book.

Once upon a time, we would sit and listen to our elders, peers - or even the wisdom of children – and soak in timeless insight and experience. Of course, we would promptly ignore it, go out, and make the same mistakes they warned us about, and then sagely nod our heads about the advice, and pass it onto the next person willing to listen.

Well, this is a whole book of those pearls of wisdom. In no way is it a complete life guide, but it is the essentials as I see them. And to be clear, just because I know the value of these things, doesn't mean I am wise enough to follow them all. Good luck in being smarter than I am!

1. Save Money

Most folks know they have to work for a living, but what many never come to realize is that you have to save money if you ever want to stop needing to work so you can live, this includes retirement.

Our modern society has come to rely on loans for so many things; we have become accustomed to not owning our homes, cars, and even our basic electronics and appliances. I recommend you stop that trend, and the best way is learn to save.

I could write a whole book on this topic alone, and many others already have. The simple math is put away a minimum of 10% of any money you make, but 20% is much better. Don't touch it. This isn't for repairing your car, vacations, or anything else. This is money so you can stop working one day.

Use coupons, shop sales, buy generic in things you can, and don't buy tons of useless stuff you don't need. People with money follow these rules, and because of it they keep more of their money.

Oh, and whenever you can, pay cash. Especially for big purchases like your car or house. At least put down big down payments. The less you pay any finance charge, the more money you save.

Travis I. Sivart

2. Pursue Your Dreams & Passions

Life is meant to be enjoyed but balanced with our responsibilities. Too many people forget that. They go to work, come home, watch TV, eat dinner, and go to bed. On their days off they spend a little money and say that this must be happiness.

When we're younger we have passion and dreams. We play instruments, dance like crazy monkeys, write poetry, want to visit every corner of the world, act in movies, parachute, dive with dolphins, and so many other things. As many people get older they forget that they can still do these things. They find excuses like; not enough time, job is too demanding, kids make it impossible, can't afford it, and tons of other reasons.

The good news is that it doesn't have to be that way; you can still find time for what you love. The bad news is that you may have to give up other things to free up money and time to be able to live your dreams. You can't spend six hours in front of the TV or computer every night if you want to learn to play an instrument or learn a new language. You can't buy that overpriced car and still afford to travel to foreign countries.

The best news is that the choice of how you spend your time and money is up to you.

3. Live Your Bucket List

A little while back someone asked me what I would put on my bucket list. It took me over a week to come up with something, because everything I thought of I had already done. Even the couple of things I thought of that I hadn't done yet, I had in the planning stages. I was living my bucket list.

This relates to the previous entry, pursuing your dreams and passions, and they go hand in hand. So many folks wait until there is – what they perceive as – almost no time left in their lives to do the cool things that they've always talked about doing.

Make your bucket list - whether you're sixteen, sixty-six, or any other age – and begin checking things off by making them happen now. If you make a new list every ten years, you'll see it change as you change.

Don't wait until you feel like you're running out of time. Begin living life to the fullest. Today plan to do something you want to do tomorrow.

4. Make Time for Friends & Family

I don't know about you, but I have been estranged from my family. I watch others with their family and it makes me happy to see the community that has decades of roots that a family gives someone. As I got older and had a son of my own, I wanted him to have that also. When I realized I couldn't do it with blood relations, I turned to my friends.

A very old adage says, 'Friends are the family which you choose', and that is the truth if you choose your friends carefully. I have had friends that have done more for me than my family ever will, and I have done the same for others.

The point is, work is fine, but it is the people in your life that make it feel full, fun, and beautiful. Objects never give the pleasure that good company that cares about you and your well-being can give. Make time to spend with your family- whether that is your parents, cousins, spouse, children, siblings, or whoever – or your friends. These are the people who make any achievement feel even better. Take care of them first and foremost.

5. Live True to Yourself, Not Others

This one can be hard to understand until you have gone through a certain amount of challenges in life; on the other hand some folks are born understanding this. The old saying of "You can't make everyone happy" is key to this. The truth is; you can't make anyone happy except yourself.

Think that's wrong? Think about when you're in a bad mood and someone tries to cheer you up. If you don't want to be cheered up, they can't make you happy. Only when you choose to let them lift your spirits do things brighten up for you. You choose to let them make you happy, thus you made yourself happy by appreciating their efforts. Without your own consent to be happy, you would've stayed miserable and cranky.

Living true to yourself means taking care of yourself, living your dreams, and allowing yourself to be happy. Don't try to find happiness in making other people's lives better. If you're living true to yourself, then the people in your life will reap those benefits as a fringe benefit. But trying to live your life to make others happy is a plan doomed to failure in the long run.

6. Work to Live, Don't Live to Work

I covered a little bit of this in the friends and family part, but now I will cover this specific point more in depth. Work is part of life and gives us many things; money to spend on necessities and frivolities, a sense of identity, a feeling of accomplishment, a sense of community and belonging, and more. But rarely is it ultimately fulfilling.

As important as work is, it is merely a tool so you may enjoy life overall. If it consumes all your time and energy, you won't have either of those things when you are with people you love and doing the things you enjoy.

Always make time to enjoy the fruits of your labor. Otherwise, what was the point of the labor?

7. Be Honest & Express Your Feelings

When dealing with life it is often easier to be happy if you simply let the people around you know what you want and how you feel about something. Hiding your feelings only leads to an explosion, of some sort, later.

It is easy to lose opportunities just because you were too shy or nervous to step up and let people know that you want it, or don't want it.

This can be a fine line, and only practice and common sense can truly guide you in this. Being honest and expressing yourself is a selective thing, and knowing when to do it is as important as doing it. Don't bludgeon or bully others just to get your way.

8. Confidence

Confidence is one of the most attractive things a person can possess. I don't mean the swagger and false egotism that makes people look at you. I mean truly understanding what you're worth, and we are all worth more than we know.

Physically, this may be as simple as pulling your shoulders back, and looking people in the eye. A firm handshake and voice helps a lot too. Speaking to the point and not beating around the bush is another way to show your confidence. Don't hem and haw, that makes folks think you don't know what you want.

9. Forgive & Forget More

Don't hold onto anger, discontentment, and emotional pain. That is the point of forgiving and forgetting. It is not the literal act of blinding yourself to someone who does bad things to you. That would be idiocy. But when you can forgive, it is a release for you. You take away the power that person has over you by removing their control over your anger or fear.

As for forgetting, this is the process of moving on, not removing the event from your memory. Don't let one event or act stop you from taking risks in that area ever again. Like with forgiving though, don't keep making the same mistake again and again, or put yourself into the same situation.

This is all about peace of mind and not carrying emotional baggage that stops you from enjoying new things, not about letting one person repeatedly abuse you. Leave that person or situation in the past, and move on. That is forgiving and forgetting.

10. Stand Up for Yourself

Standing up for yourself can take many forms. But I feel it can be summed up in one simple phrase; don't let yourself be used by others.

As a child I was smaller than the other kids, and I got picked on for it. Often this would be the bigger kid shoving me or knocking me down. I would stand right back up and look him in the eyes. Of course, I usually said something too, and then he usually knocked me down again. I am not saying this was the smartest course of action for me to take, but I did it anyway. Every single time, someone else stepped in and things settled down.

In life, it is not always that simple or obvious when you're being taken advantage of. Sometimes it is someone at work or home who asks you to do a task that isn't your responsibility. Doing it once to be nice is fine, even a good thing. But if you end up doing it every time, then they are taking advantage of you. To stand up for yourself, you don't have to create a confrontation. Sometimes it's as simple as walking away.

11. Face Your Fears

Facing your fears can be one of the most difficult things you ever do. It can take the form of sitting in a dark room, asking someone to have coffee with you, or just pushing through your anxiety to do a task that should be a simple, daily event like returning something at a store. Don't jump off a building to get over your fear of heights, but do use a step stool to get something off the top shelf.

The reason it is important to face your fears is not to banish that fear, but to show yourself that you can do it. When you want to, you can overcome anything to get something you want. This is a healthy thing.

12. Don't Pursue What Runs Away

I am a huge proponent for pursuing your dreams, and often say you can't fail unless you give up. But, some things run away from you. You'll never pet a cat if you chase it. It has to come to you, or at least meet you half way.

This advice most often applies to matters of the heart. If you make your interest known, and that person doesn't meet you half way, then don't pursue them. They will only run faster. And if they appear to be interested, but retreat every time you come closer to them (not necessarily physically), then they are probably playing games with you for their own ego's sake. Or they don't know how to express that they aren't interested and don't want to hurt you. Don't pursue that. Move on and find something that is healthier.

13. Live in the Moment

This is so important. We all have a past, and it's good to reminisce, and learn from our previous successes and failures. We all have a future, and it's good to plan and hope for what's coming. But you can't live in the past or the future. That's self-destructive.

Living in the moment is a great way to release stress. Most stress comes from regret of the past, or fear of the future. By realizing what's going on right now, right this second, you can enjoy life.

14. Be Aware of Your Surroundings

The reason this is important advice is two-fold. One, being aware of your surroundings allows you to avoid dangers. That may be tripping over the bump in the sidewalk, or avoiding the shady looking character searching for trouble. Two, it allows you to enjoy what's around you; whether it's birds singing, a pretty cloud, a funny sign, or anything else that may bring a moment of joy.

It's the little things in life that make up the big things.

15. Learn to Listen

Learning when to stop talking and listen instead is an invaluable skill that will serve you well your whole life. This isn't tuning out while daydreaming so the other person can ramble on about crap you don't care about. This is active listening, which means mentally going through the information as it is given to you.

This can be used in school, at work, or even with a friend. It allows you to glean more information, ask leading questions to dig deeper, and most importantly, help someone by actually listening to what they are saying and their meaning.

So many people never have a conversation. Instead, they catch one tidbit of information, then mentally loop the response they want to give, and aren't listening at all. They are just waiting for their chance to spout more crap. Most folks who talk want to be heard. That's all they want. They want to know you heard what they are saying. Their fears, dreams, silly jokes, crazy ideas, extreme opinions, and whatever else they spout out.

Active listening deepens the bond between two people, and gives so much to the speaker, as well as the listener.

16. Know What You Want

How can you ever do anything you want, or succeed if you never even know what you want? Perhaps right now, you're muttering that you do know what you want. Well? Go on, tell yourself what you want. Start with today, what do you want out of this day, or what did you want to accomplish? Now what about this month? This year? The next decade? In fifty years?

Yes, get all that info from yourself. Oh wait, let me reassure you – it's ok to not know. Realizing that you don't know is the first step to figuring it out. Also, allow the answers to change as you grow and change. But without a goal, aka knowing what you want, how can you accomplish anything?

This goes from something simple like; I want to make one person smile, or I want to make money today, to huge amazing things like; I want to write a book, or travel to another country. Obviously, some things can be daily goals, others are longer term goals and deserve to be given more time to come to fruition.

In the simplest of reason to know what you want – even if it is just pizza, or Chinese, for dinner – is because people respect and follow someone who knows what they want. Choose to lead, or decide to follow someone else who knows what they want.

17. Stay Clean, Dress Neatly

When I was sixteen and living on my own with a twenty-seven year old roommate in New York, he said something that stuck with me; always look your best, even if you're covered in paint and wearing work clothes. See, we did painting, tile working, wallpapering, and other such tasks. And I would watch this man, even when a mess from working, step up to another person and have an air of confidence that made the other person notice him.

I know I already covered confidence, but this is an extension of that. Dress neatly, let's start with that. This means don't look like crap. How do I explain this in one page? Look your best within the circumstances you are in. Tuck in your shirt, stand up straight, wear clean clothes, or whatever you can to show folks that you know what you're doing. Never be the slob. Slovenly behavior or appearance gives the impression that you don't care about yourself; and if you don't care about yourself, why should anyone else? Even in the torn jeans, rebellious phase, you can still be clean and neat. That may sound like it is at odds with one another, but it isn't.

18. Learn to Speak

This is so important; I cannot express this vague and confusing, what-the-hell-do-you-mean concept enough. So, let's see if I can explain it so you get it.

When I was fourteen years old, a young lady and I were walking down the street. I was complimenting her, and said, "Your voice is like, I don't know, I can't describe it." And she replied, "Yes you can, Travis, you can describe anything." And I realized she was right. So to close the story, I said her voice sounded like a pink, fluffy cloud.

The point is that knowing how to express yourself verbally is invaluable. You don't have to be elegant or poetic, just able to do it. How do you accomplish this? I will give you a few ideas.

Slow down. Collect your thoughts, organize them, and then lay them out in front of the other person in a very clear manner.

Keep it simple. Don't go into the details too much, others will grow bored and begin picking it apart. Let them create the details that work for them. The point is to get your meaning across, not make a long dissertation to make them be in awe of you.

Realize when someone isn't listening. When you feel you must repeat yourself, when they don't follow your whole thought but argue one point you made in the beginning, or a bazillion other things… stop talking. They aren't listening. You made your point, let it rest.

Travis I. Sivart

19. Be Prepared

Got a handkerchief? No? Why not? They're small, compact, and have a bunch of uses. They can be used to clean a windshield, mop up a spill, bind a wound, blow your nose when you can't find a tissue or napkin, but the most common use is to give it (not lend, but give) to a woman who is crying.

Being prepared is a wide and varied piece of advice, which I would clarify with, you cannot be prepared for every eventuality. But you can carry a few things that allow you to be ready for many different things, and this goes for men or women, (even the hanky thing). In the physical side of things; carry a pocketknife, loose change, small screwdriver, lighter, or anything else you think you may have some use for more than four times a year. Ok, don't go crazy, but it's easy enough to have a pen and paper ready as opposed to other things. Have a jack in your car, a cell phone allows you to have a calculator, compass, etc. Multi-tools are cheap and portable.

You can never be prepared for everything, but you can have a general readiness.

20. Know Three Clean Jokes

This is something I used to phrase as, know three jokes you could tell to your grandmother. But today's grandmothers aren't the same saintly, silver-haired, innocent, little old ladies that we used to think of in my childhood. In this current day and age, they may also be silver-haired, tattooed, raise-a-shot-and-drink-to-your-health, tell-you-to-go-screw-yourself, woman that is the modern strong lady.

So, I advise that you know three clean jokes that you can tell among strangers that may be kindergarteners, church-going believers, or whatever.

Why should you do this? Because humor is universal, and creating a bond with laughter is invaluable. Now, go learn about the horse that walked into the bar, and the bartender said, "Why the long face?"

21. Understand Your Goals, Large & Small

Oh, where do I start on this? Ok, so I mentioned this in a couple of other places. Let me break it down; goals are not one huge thing, they are many small things. Quick example; you want to skydive and parachute. This is more than one step, such as; save money, research a place, set up an appointment, do the pre-jump stuff, do the jump, post to social media, etc.

What I just showed you is a large goal, broken up into many smaller goals. A large goal can become overwhelming and intimidating. But if you break it into manageable bites, it's easier to digest and accomplish.

My point is don't let a large goal become too much for you. Break it into smaller goals, which make you feel like you have succeeded in each step, and encourages you to complete the larger achievement.

Travis I. Sivart

22. Clean as You Go

Really, follow this as a rule in everything you do. I'll compare it to your home, apartment, and even your car. Don't let things pile up, they become a mess. If you put things in the trash, and take it out before it's full, then you never have trash everywhere. If you organize things – dirty clothes, mail, dirty dishes, or whatever – and take care of them on a regular basis (ok, I mean daily) then they never can overwhelm you.

Spending five minutes to clean your dishes is easier than thirty minutes with an overflowing sink. Taking in one fast food bag full of trash from the day's travel is easier than digging through a pile of trash in your car floorboard that comes to your knees, etc.

This goes for all kinds of things, not just your home and car. This rule applies to emotional and mental issues too. Don't let them build up to overwhelming proportions. But only you can take care of it before it becomes a tidal wave and makes you want to run for a hiding place.

23. Avoid Extremes & Excess

In all things, avoid extremes and excess. I've had too many friends ruin their lives to drugs, food, video games, or obsessive behavior over their love interest because of extremes and excess.

Don't do it.

Realize a healthy life is a balance. There's not all or nothing, black or white, right or wrong. Everything is made up of layers and spectrums and not just two things.

I can't make this simpler than I have. If you don't get it in what you just read, then enjoy the recovery from your chosen addiction.

24. Succeed & Fail with Grace

I guarantee you will succeed in some things, and fail in others. This may be as simplistic as a game or discussion, or as complex as a career or a love relationship. Learn to succeed and fail without creating drama around what you've done.

Some folks feel the need to draw attention to their selves and let folks know how urgent, important, and paramount their peak or valley in life has been. Don't be that person. Your friends will celebrate or commiserate these events, as appropriate, but if you think the world needs to know or care, you have just crossed a line that will make you more of a tabloid headline than an emotionally excited or interesting individual.

Personal success or failure is meant to be supported by your inner circle, not the whole world. The sooner you learn that, the better your support structure will be. By the way, ringing that bell too often is akin to the boy that cried wolf. Don't do it just because you have the urge to get a little attention, no matter the cost.

25. Use Manners & Common Courtesy

Please, thank you, yes sir, no ma'am, holding the door for a stranger, etc. goes further than you may ever know. For the most part this is a seamless and invisible habit, a thankless task. But in the long run, those most often around you will form an opinion about your grace and personal character.

More importantly is the effect is has on you as an individual, and your own self-worth. Don't hesitate to be courteous for your own sake. If that doesn't make sense, then let me put it this way; this is a silent investment in your own character and self-worth. Be the person who finds small pleasure in helping others in inconsequential ways. Because, it actually makes a huge difference in your unconscious view of yourself.

26. Breathe, Hydrate, & Sleep

Three of the most basic things in any animal - and we are still animals no matter what we may think – is to drink plenty, sleep enough, and breathe deeply.

Sleep is one of the most important things to thinking clearly and being ready to face any challenge the day may present.

Drinking enough WATER – not soda, coffee, or whatever – makes you physically able to function.

Breathing; oh, where do I start with this? Getting the proper amount of oxygen to your body effects everything you do. Breathe deeply when stressed or anxious, making yourself take multiple – at least ten – deep breaths allows you to think clearly and respond better.

This is science, folks. Look it up. Sleep enough, drink enough, and breathe right.

27. Time Management

Being successful in anything - personal, professional, or anything else – is time management. Whether you're waiting tables, setting up a home, or writing a book, it's a matter of realizing that there are only so many hours in the day, and so many minutes in each hour.

Setting your schedule so you're the most productive you can be is the key to being who you want to be. There is nothing wrong with wasting time enjoying pleasure activities, as long as it is balanced with doing the things that move you forward in life.

Make lists or schedules, and sticking to them is the key to getting what you want. No one else will do this for you.

27 Thoughts on
Phrases That
Changed My Life

Travis I. Sivart

27 Thoughts on Phrases That Changed My Life

Dedication

This book is for me, but dedicated to all those people, events, and life lessons that gave me what I needed to carry on.

Introduction

Like everyone, I've gone through my personal, difficult moments in life. These are phrases that inspired me in those challenging times. These phrases have been on Post-It Notes on my monitor, on 3x5 cards tucked in my sun visor, scrawled on my dry erase boards, or written a dozen times in various steno pads as I transferred notes from one to the other.

Some of the wisdom is from others, famous sayings that have lasted the ages. Others are from movies, just key quotes that stuck in my head when I needed that tidbit of advice. And still others are from my own experiences and are my words.

I often analyze my situation and look for a succinct answer that sums the issues up nicely; or a reminder to make sure I don't get myself into the same problem again in the future.

These ideas are nothing new. They've been around since we began inventing philosophy. Use what helps you and don't worry about the rest. I hope these 27 phrases can help inspire and caution you as effectively as they have me.

1. That's what average people do; I don't want to be average.

Travis I. Sivart

Average people make up most of our population, that's why they're average. These everyday folks who wake up, go to work, come home, watch TV and check their computers, eat dinner, and go to bed are the core of our society and I have immense respect for them.

But, I don't want to be like them. I tried it, and it didn't work out. It was like committing suicide of my mind and personality. I tried very hard, but just couldn't do it. I failed at being normal.

Instead, I dream wild dreams, then pursue them. I take risks that sensible people wouldn't consider. I learn new skills just to do something one time. I stay up too late to experience something, and go to work dead tired the next day. I don't have the best car, newest phone, or get new living room furniture every couple of years. But I've gone to Europe on a shoestring, painted every wall in my house a different color, dress in a tux and tails to go out for fast food, and wrote books about whatever strikes my fancy.

I live my dreams and fantasies, which is not what the average person does. But, I don't want to be average.

2. Argue your limitations, and they are yours.
Richard Bach, Illusions

This is from a book I read in my mid-teens, and it changed my view of life. It was a serious, honest-to-God, life-changing moment. I've reread the book every couple of years and remind myself of what I knew as a teen, and perhaps even learn something new as my perspective changes.

We all have limits, and it's good to know them. But that doesn't mean we can't push our boundaries and comfort zones. Arguing for your limitations is one sure way to ensure defeat before you even start. Self-imposed restrictions are one sure way to never make your dreams come true. Don't do that to yourself.

Travis I. Sivart

3. Stress and tension are self-inflicted.
Travis I. Sivart

I worry. Most people do. I sometimes get into a cycle of thinking about situations or circumstances so that I get tension headaches. This isn't a pressure put on me by anyone else. I do it to myself.

Then one day I realized my mind creates that stress and tension. I consciously recognized this and set it aside. It comes back occasionally, and I have to do it again.

It isn't easy to do this, but by being aware that you are causing yourself harm, you can stop this cycle. Some folks cut themselves, and this is an emotional and mental way of doing the same thing.

Face your issues, take care of what you can, plan for the rest. But don't dwell on the things you cannot change at this very moment. Stop cutting yourself.

Travis I. Sivart

4. Today is the first day of the rest of your life.

Charles Dederich

A phrase made popular in the 1970s, though I'm sure the concept was around long before ol' Chuck came up with it as a slogan.

We wake up every morning to face a new day, and every new day is another chance to succeed. It can be a fresh beginning, if you allow it to be. More than that, you have to put your mental foot down and decide that it's a clean slate, any hardships or failures in the past can be let go of, and you can move forward.

Don't be your own anchor to hold yourself back. Don't let your past failures decide that you cannot have future success. Start new, now, today.

Travis I. Sivart

5. If you don't choose your purpose, your life will never have one.

Travis I. Sivart

Many people seek a purpose in their life. The secret is that you get to decide what this is. This was said well in the Classic Billy Crystal and Jack Palance comedy, City Slickers.

In a scene, Billy's character was frustrated and Jack's character asked, "Do you know what the meaning of life is?"

Billy shook his head, and Jack held up a gloved finger and said, "One thing, this."

"Your finger?" Billy asked.

"No, it's one thing." Jack growled.

"What is it?" Billy shouted.

"That's up to you to decide." Jack answered.

Maybe I'm paraphrasing the conversation, but that's the gist of it. You decide what your purpose is, what your goal will be, and what's important to you. Then you make your life have purpose and meaning with that one thing.

6. Just keep swimming.

Dory, Finding Nemo

A classic kid's movie from Pixar, but it held a gem of wisdom from the absent-minded, tag-along, comedy-relief friend, Dory. She even sang a song about it, "Just Keep Swimming."

In life, you can't give up, or not move forward, and expect to have things come to you. Though that may work occasionally, it isn't a sure thing. The only sure way to continue to have a life be interesting and to succeed is to keep moving forward. I reflect on this idea in a couple of other thoughts in this book.

It's important to not give up. Giving up is the only guaranteed way to fail.

7. The right word can mean the world.
Travis I. Sivart

This is a quote I put in the very first book I published. As an author, it holds a lot of truth. In the literal sense, many words can mean the world. Globe, Earth, biosphere, planet, etc. In the non-literal way, which is the manner I mean for this phrase, just a single word can change someone's life.

I'm usually an upbeat fellow, but one day in my teens, I was walking along the sidewalk in sunny Florida with my head down and my hands shoved in my pockets. I was in a foul mood. I passed a middle-aged woman. Usually I'd make eye contact, smile, and give a pleasantry. That day, I was in no mood to deal with anyone. As we passed, she said, "Hello."

That single word struck me. I muttered hello back to her. Then I walked with my head up. I smiled. I pulled my hands out of my pockets and put my shoulders back. Her single word changed my day and my mood.

My point is, a single word from you can change someone's day. A phone call or message can improve their week. A conversation can change their entire outlook. Don't ignore this ability to influence others in a positive way. And don't use it to create negative results.

8. I've wrestled with reality for thirty-five years, Doc, and I'm happy to state I finally won out over it.

Elwood P. Dowd, Harvey

Reality can be a bitch. Life can be hard. But you have to let it be that way to you. You have to set your mind to it to make this happens.

Of course, you have to also set your mind to let life be fun. To make reality what you want, a positive environment, you have to wrestle with it. Shape it and make it what you want. This takes time and effort. Don't let it bear you down. Fight for your reality to be something you want to live in.

Choose to surround yourself with things that make you happy. Do things that make you feel good and appreciate the things you have.

9. If I sit, my feet ache; if I walk, they rejoice.
Travis I. Sivart

I first said this in my mid-teens. Most folks didn't understand what I meant by it, though. I will explain it to you now. If I stay still in life and don't move forward, I feel like I'm missing something. And I am, I'm missing success and adventure in life.

When I move forward in life, and attempt to do things, I find I'm happy. I look forward to what the next day brings. I crave to create something. This may be a story, a painting, a good meal, or just to clean and organize my home.

Any way it goes, moving forward creates a positive reaction in me, but doing nothing makes me ache inside for something else.

Travis I. Sivart

10. Attitude: The difference between ordeal and adventure.

Travis I. Sivart

Life throws challenges at us. If we're smart and/or motivated, then most of them are self-created. But either way, we face trials almost every day. And it's our attitude as we deal with them that decides if they're troublesome ordeals, or exciting adventures.

If you stress and suffer every time something comes up, life becomes a tribulation. You spend so much time worrying about what you are facing; you don't bother to see past it to what you can have once you beat it.

Most things that happen to us that make us upset or frustrated…if it happened in a movie or TV show you were watching, you'd know the person will overcome it and get the reward waiting on the other side. You sit forward in your chair, excited, wanting to know how your favorite character will win out over whatever it is they're facing.

Why not do that in your own life? Smile, roll up your sleeves, take charge, and put the work in, knowing you'll get something worthwhile once it's passed.

11. Never give up, never surrender!
Galaxy Quest

Galaxy Quest was a great movie, full of exciting challenges and funny lines. But the one line that stuck with me is the catchphrase of the crew: "Never give up, never surrender!"

It means that, well, just what it says. Don't lay down and give up. Don't let life beat you. Anything can be overcome and beat if you just don't give up. It's pretty simple.

I've used this as a mantra when things are particularly tough for me. I find myself muttering it as I drive, reminding myself that I can't be beat if I don't give up, if I don't surrender. It's helped me grit my teeth and push forward, and through, anything I was dealing with.

12. Mourn not what you have lost, but rather, rejoice in what you have.

Travis I. Sivart

Life is ever changing. One of my many stepfathers used to say, "Nothing is constant, except change." Life is full of things and people that come and go. You'll lose things in this life, that's a fact.

I've lost friends and family to the ebb and flow of life. Some have died, some just fade away. It makes me sad until I realize I still have others around me that care. And by focusing on what I have, it makes me realize the value of what I still retain, and I'm grateful for that.

I've had many jobs, homes, and belongings. I've lost more than what I have, but I have what I need. The things that are gone were wonderful when I had them, but to disregard what I currently have to mourn what I no longer can have, seems just silly and harmful to my mental state.

I still remember these people and things from time to time, but I do it with a wistful smile, enjoying the memory. Then I go and enjoy what I have around me right now.

13. Whether you think you can or you can't, you're right.

Henry Ford

Henry Ford, the man known for making the first mass-produced automobile, as well as being a prosperous businessman, was also a wise man. He coined this phrase, meaning that you decide if you can succeed before you even start.

It's your own belief in yourself that ultimately decides if you flourish or fail. If you move forward expecting to bomb, you will. It's pretty much a guarantee.

A can-do attitude paves the way to achieving whatever it is you're attempting to do.

14. Here's to our vices; may we choose them, and never be a slave to them!

Travis I. Sivart

I enjoy a drink, a pipe or cigar, a good movie, and the occasional video game. I love to take a day and waste it sitting on the couch, with my feet up and cats purring in my lap. But none of these things will ever be a stumbling block to me succeeding.

I don't have addictions, though they have reared their ugly head on occasion. I don't allow my vices to have so much control over me I can't put them down, walk away, and do something I want to do.

15. A master has failed more times than a beginner has tried.

Hindi Saying

We're all beginners at some point. We may have a talent for one particular thing, but it doesn't mean we're great at it, just that we have a knack for it.

Many people give up when a certain skill doesn't come easy. I don't know if our society is more self-entitled now—as many would claim—or if it's always been that way, but you can't just pick up a new thing and be a master of it. You have to work, and work long and hard, to become truly great at a thing.

Popular culture says you're a master once you have done something for ten-thousand hours. That's over a year's worth of work, if you're doing it twenty-four hours a day. But we rarely work over eight hours a day, five days a week. That means it takes over five years of full-time work to become a master. Now, apply that logic to a skill that others would call a hobby, like painting, music, or writing. These things would take much more than five years, because we rarely partake of our hobbies as frequently or at the same length as we do work.

If you love something, though, work at it. Practice it. Devote time and energy to it. You will become skilled in time; sometimes slowly, sometimes with an epiphany that lets you grow in leaps and bounds. The bottom line is to keep trying until you are a master, then try some more.

Travis I. Sivart

16. Small blessings and silver linings are all we have some days. Learn to cherish them.
Travis I. Sivart

Life can be harsh, come at you quick, and overwhelm you with the sheer mass of challenges. To help keep your psychological equilibrium and emotional balance, appreciating the small things in life is essential.

Every day, we have dozens of small successes; getting out of bed, hygiene routines, a laugh with a friend, seeing something that makes you smile or giggle, a delicious treat, and any of the other things we see, do, or experience on a daily basis.

Remembering these is important. Appreciating them is even more important. It's so easy to only recall the bad or annoying things at the end of the day. But we must pull the good things to the front, and move on from what brings us down.

Make a practice of doing this. When you remember something from your day, your brain produces the same chemicals—good or bad—that were produced when you first experienced the event. If you ate something nasty during the day, and something wonderful later, which flavor would you rather experience again once you're home?

The same goes for remembering.

17. A smooth sea never made a skilled sailor.
Franklin D. Roosevelt

Adversity builds character is another way of saying this. Which isn't completely true; but for most folks that fight their way through problems and come out the other side, they gain a new way of looking at things.

By facing problems, issues, challenges, trials, and tribulations in life, it teaches us to see beyond that and keep our eye on what we're trying to accomplish.

Also, by facing these challenges, you build your skill set. This may be a physical skill set associated with an activity (such as painting, repairing cars, or any number of things) or it may be less tangible and take form in a social skill set, such as when you deal with difficult people.

The bottom line is that facing issues and overcoming them allows you to grow and become more skilled in ways that only experience can provide.

18. Life isn't as serious as my mind makes it out to be.

Travis I. Sivart

I sometimes need to stop, take a deep breath, and remind myself to calm down and everything will be ok. On occasion, I'll compare life to a movie and encourage myself to see it from the frame of reference of the audience, knowing it will end well, and once this scene has passed, it'll no longer matter.

This isn't to say I should have a completely flippant attitude about what's happening in my world. But instead, to not allow the drama of a single moment to cloud my view of the larger picture of my life.

Life isn't a joke, but you'll enjoy it more if you learn to laugh more often than you worry.

19. What truly creates change is changing your perspective and perception.
Travis I. Sivart

Changing your point of view is mind expanding. Seeing the world through someone else's eyes is something that can alter your life and how you treat people forever.

Your perspective is limited, and your perception of your perspective further categorizes, boxes, labels, defines, and confines what you see, hear, and experience in any form. When you look at something, let's use a house, for example, you see it and experience it. If you move further away, you can see its surroundings and how those affect it. If you move closer, you can see details showing care or abuse. If you walk all the way around the house, you can see the yard, neighbors, the back door, and so many other things you may not have seen from the porch. And if you move inside it, it's a whole other world.

This is the same for people, places, events, experiences, or anything else. Changing your perspective allows you a different, and unique, view of whatever it is you're observing. Changing your perception allows you to see it from the inside, exposing so much more than you can see from the outside. Knowledge and understanding are the key to change.

20. Expectation is the root of all heartache.
William Shakespeare

This is a simple truth. If you have a predesignated concept of what will happen, you've already set yourself up to be disappointed.

There's a difference between working towards a goal with likely results, and having expectations with no acceptance of the possibility of something else happening.

This is true when it comes to projects, relationships, work, or anything else. Leave possibilities open and it'll pleasantly surprise you when things turn out differently than you thought, rather than being heartbroken when they don't turn out the way you expected.

21. Approval comes at a price. Make sure you're willing to pay the latter before seeking the former.

Travis I. Sivart

If you run around hoping to gain other people's approval, that means you're doing something for them rather than yourself. It costs you something to gain another person's appreciation, gratitude, or endorsement.

It may be your time while you try to do things that please the other person (whether that's your boss, a friend, a family member, your significant other, or just some stranger), or it could be your resources, your pride, or even other friendships.

Before you try to gain someone's favor by doing whatever it is you think they want, or what would please them; consider the cost you'll pay for that.

Travis I. Sivart

22. A journey of a thousand miles begins with a single step.

Lao Tzu

Dory said it well, "Just keep swimming." In Galaxy Quest they said, "Never give up, never surrender!" It's an ageless saying, and for some folks (like myself) a life philosophy.

This boils down to "you can't get anywhere without moving forward." To achieve anything you MUST move, keep moving, one foot in front of the other, don't stop, don't give up, and keep on keeping on.

It's such a common saying in so many forms that it's often just assimilated into our cultural surroundings and we lose sight of the value of the wisdom the thought holds.

To recap; you can't succeed in anything without doing something.

23. It's the ride you remember, not the wait in line.

Travis I. Sivart

When my son was just a wee lad of seven or eight years of age, I took him to Disney World. We were standing in a long and winding line; it was hot, and he was waiting patiently. I don't know if he overheard someone complaining, but he suddenly said, "When you get home from the park, it's the ride you remember, not the wait in line."

In life, we often find ourselves impatiently waiting for the next thing to happen. First, enjoy that wait as a break between the peaks and valleys of life. Second, at the end of your life—when you look back across the years—you aren't going to remember the slow times, the waiting, the downtime. Instead, you'll remember the ride. The peaks and valleys of life.

So when in a holding pattern, relax. It's ok. You'll have plenty of rides to remember.

Travis I. Sivart

Travis I. Sivart

Travis I. Sivart

Travis I. Sivart

24. Success is measured not so much by the position that one has reached in life as by the obstacles he has to overcome while trying to succeed.

Booker T. Washington

I've known many successful people in life, and in almost every instance, the more they overcame to reach where they were...was matched by the level of respect they garnered from others around them.

A marathon runner who's in their twilight years and has overcome a stroke will often gain more attention than a young man in his twenties who runs the same marathon. The same can be applied to someone who made their way through college or university by earning money or scholarships rather than someone who was given money and didn't have to hold a job while earning their degree.

If you want to measure your success, look at how much you've done, how much you've worked, overcome, or fought to get where you are. It stands out and shows passion and drive above and beyond what another may have who had to do less to get to the same place.

25. When you know you're dreaming, you can change and influence your dreams. Waking is no different.

Travis I. Sivart

This is a tough concept to wrap your head around, similar to not taking life too seriously because no one gets out alive. Or becoming so wrapped up in a problem that you can't see past it, and you end up suffering because you won't let yourself do anything else.

When you're dreaming and being chased by a monster, if you can realize that you're dreaming, you can make choices that you couldn't otherwise. You can choose to fight, to fly, to turn the monster into a bunny. Real life can be very similar, and you can choose how to perceive things, and realize all things are temporary and can be changed through your own will and effort.

26. Focus – Commitment – Pure Will

John Wick

This is a philosophy introduced in an action movie, and it is a perfect recipe for succeeding in life. The main character does things no other man can, through these three things.

Focus. Giving your full attention to something allows you to analyze it in ways that partial attention does not. It lets you look at things, finding other options, ways, and methods of handling it. Or it allows you to fully commit to the task.

Commitment. You're much less likely to complete any task if you're not committed to succeeding at it. Going "all in" gives you effort and energy to overcoming obstacles, finding that creative drive, or making whatever it is to do what you want to do.

Pure Will. Not giving up is key to succeeding in any task, no matter how small or monumental. Having the willpower to work out, lose weight, write a book, get that job, finish that course, or whatever it is you're doing is how you see things through when all your other inspirations have faded.

27. Admit your worth; to yourself, and to others.

Travis I. Sivart

So many people, especially creative people, don't recognize their own worth, skills, or ability. They're often shy, self-demeaning, or just don't want to brag.

There's a difference between confidence and being arrogant and tooting your own horn. The first step is admitting to yourself that what you offer is worth having. You have value, and others appreciate it.

Many times, though, people are so busy with their own lives that they fail to recognize the value others offer. There's nothing wrong with being proud of yourself, as long as it isn't at the expense of others. There's never a need to elevate yourself by putting others down.

But you should always feel comfortable talking about your own achievements and worth when appropriate.

27 Thoughts on
Profound
Sayings

Travis I. Sivart

27 Thoughts on Profound Sayings

Dedication

This book is dedicated to all those great folks who I met at countless events, conventions, parties, online, and so many other places, that love words as much as I do.

Introduction

I grew up with people quoting wise sayings from bygone eras, or maybe it was just stuff the crazy old man at the gas station would say. When I was very young, many of these didn't make much sense, and by the time I got older I had heard them so many times that I never even thought about the meanings. Until I grew up and had heard these phrases countless times in many variations, only then did I realize these were staples of wisdom.

I have decided to take what I consider the most important of these and explain them, because what we see and hear too often become assimilated into our environment and we no longer see them as special and interesting.

I think these pearls of wisdom should be cherished, and I hope that this book makes you also cherish the value of these one-line sayings.

1. Those Who Fit In, Rarely Stand Out

You have a couple of choices in life on how to present yourself. The first is to conform and fit in. It is a safe choice, with little judgement and often allows you to be fully accepted by those around you. The second is to be more than what everyone else is - this doesn't mean rebelling for the sake of being different, it is so much more than that – and be yourself in the truest form.

Standing out means you show your unique nature, ideas, talents, differences, or whatever. People who do this are the movers and shakers, the trendsetters, and perhaps most importantly, the ones that change the world in large and small ways.

Standing out takes extreme courage and a lot of emotional and mental stamina. It helps to have the ability to not care what others think, but still be able to look at yourself with a critical eye (otherwise you may just be an attention-seeking, self-centered jerk). But if you can do this right, you can do more than change the world – you can change a single person's whole reality by being a positive influence.

2. Be True to Yourself

So many of us, myself included at times, have tried to please everyone around us. And I speak from experience when I say that no one ends up happy from that sort of behavior. You might be able to do it for a short time, but in the long run, it is a recipe for disaster.

Being true to yourself is not about being selfish, greedy, or taking from anyone else. Instead, it is about making yourself happy and successful in your endeavors in life, and also being honest with yourself about yourself. If you can be happy - truly happy - with yourself and who you are and what you are doing, then others will be attracted to you and gravitate to you.

Petty people will talk about you, put you down, and judge you. And that's ok, it is just who they are, and they are more concerned with you than themselves – thus, not being true to themselves. You do your thing, and life will present opportunities and you will be so much happier.

3. Many a Slip Between the Cup & the Lip

Variations: Shit Happens.

When you are on the road to success you will not make it in the first few steps, or often even in the first hundred steps. The point of this saying is to let you know that it is ok to have setbacks, screw-ups, failures, and so on. The point is that eventually you will get where you're going, and accomplish what it is that you set out to do, so don't give up. Giving up is for losers, trying again is for winners.

4. Know Thyself

The hardest thing is being introspective and knowing your own hopes, fears, wants, desires, and goals. It takes a lot of damn work! But, take it from me, it is so worth it. And the hard work that follows to do what it is you want to do, to get where you want to go, and accomplish the incredible things you want to do, is so worth it.

Dig deep, explore your light side, dark side, and wishy-washy middle. Learn your own strengths and weaknesses, and admit to them. There is nothing wrong with it; in fact, it will only make you the better and stronger person once you know these things about yourself.

5. The Show Must Go On

Variations: Never Give Up, Never Surrender! One Step at a Time. No Quarter, No Mercy.

An old showbiz adage, but it applies to so many things other than stage or film. I recall Dory in *Finding Nemo* saying, "Just keep swimming!" and it means the same thing. Don't stop, just keep trying.

You cannot fail until you stop trying. So, to never fail all you have to do is try again. Also, no matter the setback, push forward until you achieve your goal. Nothing else in life can be more true. Of course, some folks might quote the phrase, "Know when to give up", but that is another entry that isn't in this book, and for pessimists. Unless your stalking someone who isn't interested, then just stop that crap.

6. Walk a Mile in Another's Shoes

Life is unique for each and every one of us – including you – just like everyone else! You cannot ever totally know what someone else is going through, unless you have gone through the exact same thing.

This is all about empathy, which is the ability to relate to someone. The drama-prone will argue that someone can never know the depths that they endure, but I assure you that they are just seeking attention. But you do need some basis of comparison before you can understand someone's problems.

Never assume that you really relate, let the other person bear their burden, but do know that you may sympathize without having experienced something specific.

7. The Journey of a Thousand Miles Begins With One Step

You cannot finish something until you begin it. It really is that simple. No matter what you want to accomplish, you cannot do that until you start down the path that leads to it, for good or ill. I encourage the good reasons, as opposed to the bad ones; such as drug addiction.

If you ever want to do something, just do it (to quote a famous advertising campaign) and move forward in your plans. Without starting, there is no success.

8. Don't Cry Over Spilled Milk

You sometimes fail. It's that simple. Don't spend too much time lamenting that point, just move on and forward. If you use all your energy boo-hooing over not succeeding, then you won't have time to succeed.

See the previous mention of not giving up.

Travis I. Sivart

9. Lie, Steal, & Cheat

A great Irish toast, usually done at weddings, and it goes something like this:

"May you never steal, lie, or cheat. But if you must steal, then steal away my sorrows. And if you must lie, lie with me all the nights of my life. And if you must cheat, then please cheat death, because I couldn't live a day without you."

But it holds a lot of meaning. Be honest in life, and give yourself to those you love. It makes life worth it.

10. Nose to the Grindstone

Back to the grind is another way to look at it. Working hard is how you get things in life.

Now this particular phrase comes from hardworking blacksmiths who would use their rounded wheel of a grindstone, keeping it spinning using a foot petal like old sewing machines, and leaning over to watch the blade they were sharpening to keep the edge smooth and clean.

It teaches the lesson of watching what you're doing with an intensity that lends itself to perfection in your task. It also leads you to focusing on that task, and keeping at it until it's done.

A well-used phrase that many folks have forgotten to look for the value within it.

11. Take Time to Smell the Flowers

Life is made of moments. Many people are so busy waiting for the big moments, they forget to enjoy the small things in life.

Stopping to smell the flowers is a way to remind you that all the big things in life – the long journeys, big events, monumental moments – are made up of many, many smaller ones. And you need to appreciate those small things. Look for the beauty every day, smell the flowers and soak up the millions of things that so many miss because they're too busy waiting for the next big thing (or lamenting the passing of some past thing) to truly enjoy life.

Travis I. Sivart

12. A Bird In the Hand Is Worth Two In the Bush

Don't gamble what you have for a chance that you will probably miss. Appreciate what you have. If you have worked hard and made something (as in you caught one bird and are holding it), don't toss it aside for a long shot (such as two birds hiding in the bush a bit away from you).

In all likelihood, you will let go of what you have and not get the other thing that you thought would be bigger or better.

This doesn't mean that you shouldn't try for bigger and better things, it only means don't give up what you have for a maybe.

13. Youth Is Wasted On the Young

As we age, we realize how much we did, and how much we didn't do. It is not so much about wisdom of experience, but often more about having regrets of not taking the chances and opportunities we were presented with when we were younger and full of energy, hope… and perhaps not so bitter or realistic as we are at later ages in life.

For you young folks out there; try that thing, take that risk, talk to that person, go on that trip. Go and do all the things. You are more likely to regret not doing things than regretting what you did do.

14. Time Flies When Having Fun

When you are occupied, especially while having fun, your mind and body are busy doing without a chance to be concerned with the passing of time. So you often don't notice such things when you're doing something you love.

When you are idle, you notice the passage of time, seeking something meaningful in the emptiness of waiting. But when you're doing, time flies.

And as you get older, time has a lot more meaning than when you're younger.

15. All Who Wander Are Not Lost

There is a charm in meandering. Wandering is an activity, and a learning experience all of its own.

Sometimes you don't need a plan or a set direction. This is how you often discover new, and unexpected things, by just going where the wind blows you.

It is seeking something, but nothing more specific than a new experience. And once you get the hang of wandering, it can quickly become a great path to new and exciting adventures.

16. K.I.S.S. (Keep It Simple, Stupid)

Planning everything down to the last detail is often the recipe for failure. There is an old saying that came before this, "no battle plan ever survives the first encounter with the enemy," often attributed to Colin Powell, but also to Field Marshal Helmuth Carl Bernard von Moltke (what a name!).

Basically this all means, go ahead and plan, but don't be inflexible in what happens once things begin to move. Keeping things simple allows you (and the people involved) to make better and quicker judgement calls once things are in motion.

17. Eye On the Prize

Or keep your eye on the ball is another way of saying it. This just encourages you to remember why you're doing what you're doing. Don't get caught up in the minutia, and be ready to change how you're doing things so you can reach whatever your goal is.

Don't get sidetracked or distracted and let other things pull you away from the one thing that you are aiming to achieve.

18. A Spoonful of Sugar Helps the Medicine Go Down

"You attract more flies with honey, than vinegar" is another version of this saying. If you have something you don't want to do, then perhaps a little incentive can make this a bit less difficult to swallow when doing the task.

This goes for having others (like employees, children, etc.) do things for you also. Having a reward at the end of the task, or even just giving encouraging words or praise, can often help inspire that person to do something they would normally complain about.

Travis I. Sivart

Travis I. Sivart

19. The World Is Your Oyster

You could say, "I have the world on a string," or even, "grab the world by the balls," and they would work. These are all sayings that lets you know that you can get many things, but you have to go out and get them.

No one is going to do all the things and let you have the rewards from their hard work. Also, if you do it then you will appreciate the end result so much more than if someone does it for you. It will hold more value because you worked for it.

Go out and shuck your oyster to find your pearl, reel in that string to get what's on the other end, or grab your challenge and take control so you can reap that reward!

Travis I. Sivart

20. Keep Calm and Carry On

Panic never helps. Losing control doesn't ever help you get further along. Keeping calm, staying in control, and taking that next step is the best way to achieve whatever it is you want to do.

Carrying on is important also. Never giving up, one foot in front of the other, chin up, and all that. The surest way to fail is to stop trying.

21. Birds of a Feather, Flock Together

"Like attracts like," and "You are the people you surround yourself with," are all ways of saying that the people closest to you will influence you, your world, how you behave, and your level of success.

Many people encourage others to surround themselves with people they'd like to be like, or people smarter than themselves, or whatever. The point is that we assimilate habits, behaviors, and patterns from what we see around us. So make sure the people around you are the kind of person you want to be.

Travis I. Sivart

22. Two Wrongs Don't Make a Right

Someone yells at you, you yell back. Things escalate.

In a world where we live by "an eye for an eye, everyone ends up blind."

Treating others how they treat you when it is violent, negative, aggressive, harmful, or destructive only leads to bad things.

Don't do more wrong or harmful things and expect things to get better. Find a way that is truly better and helpful instead.

Travis I. Sivart

23. No Man Is an Island

Every individual is influenced by, and influences, people around them. Whether this is as simple as interacting (or not interacting) with people at a store, dealing with co-workers, or living with your family, we all have people that rely on us or that we rely on.

Our bosses pay us, our employees do work for us, the farmer raises crops and meats, the city workers build roads, and so on. No one person can be completely alone when in a society. We all affect, and in turn are affected by, others. No one can do it all by themselves.

24. There's No Such Thing as a Free Lunch

"Everything has a price," is another way of saying this. For everything you get in life, someone had to work for it. And if you got it, and you didn't work for it then someone else did, and you may now owe them in some fashion.

Things in life don't just fall from the sky into your lap. If you want something, then working for it is how to get it.

And if you are getting things without putting the work in, you may just be using others and not be a very nice person.

In a final thought, keep in mind that sometimes just appreciating what you get is payment enough.

Travis I. Sivart

25. There's No Place Like Home

When I speak of home, I mean the home that you make for yourself. The comfortable place that you go to so you can get away from the world for a little while. This might be your house or apartment, it might a group of friends, one special person, or any number of other places.

Home is where the heart is, is another saying, and these two go hand in hand. That one special place where you are just relaxed, calm, feel safe, and comforted is a special place… and there is no other place in the world like it.

This doesn't have to be a place with blood relatives, but it can be. This doesn't have to be the town you grew up in, but it can be. Or it could be with a group of strangers, hiking up a mountain, or some other adventure.

Your home is just for you, and there no other place in the world like it for you.

26. Beauty Is In the Eye of the Beholder

Many parents proudly post, or hold up, photos of their children. They beam and ask, "Aren't they beautiful?" and the rest of us often swallow nervously, nod awkwardly, and look for the nearest escape route. Or it might be your old beat-up car, or that dilapidated cabin on a lake that you went to every summer as a kid.

These things are beautiful because of the meaning and emotional value they hold for a person, rather than any particular physical feature or attribute.

In art, music, poetry, and other creative outlets beauty is very personal and individualistic. What one finds breathtaking, others may pass over with a shrug or an eye-roll. But again, it is that personal connection that goes deeper than the surface that you see that makes it beautiful.

So love what you love, and let others love what they love. And try to smile when they make you look at it with them.

27. You Can Lead a Horse to Water, but You Can't Make It Drink

This is most often used to refer to a person who you are trying to share wisdom or knowledge with. You can share what you know or have experienced, but you can't make them heed what you're telling them.

Some things people just have to learn on their own, and no amount of leading, talking, sharing, yelling, cajoling, or other forms of enticement will make them get what you mean.

Other people just refuse to listen to lessons from others, thinking they know better and wouldn't have to learn the hard way. Perhaps they are right, but they may also be wrong.

I'm pretty sure most of us have been led to water more than once, and refused to drink.

Travis I. Sivart

About the Author

Travis I. Sivart is a prolific author of Fantasy, Science Fiction, Social DIY, and more. He's created The Traverse Reality, a shared universe that connects his cyberpunk, fantasy, and steampunk worlds, with characters his readers love.

Travis I. Sivart has been writing and telling stories since he was a young child. Perhaps it was inevitable that he would call grappling with words and language a career—and loving every moment. He is privileged to share his work with a large and welcoming audience. Get in touch to discover more about his work, writing process, and future endeavors.

You can sometimes find him live-streaming the writing and editing of his latest project from his home in Central Virginia, surrounded by too many cats.

You can get a free book, and discover Travis's other series, podcasts, live-streams, social media, and more at www.TravisSivart.com.

Travis I. Sivart

If you enjoyed this book…

Please let others know by reviewing it on Amazon or Goodreads, and let others know your thoughts!

Other series by Travis I. Sivart

The Steampunk Cycle

An anthology of automatons and airships, bustles and beasts, corsets and curses, dandies and dastardly deeds awaits you as you explore tales of terror, mystery, and adventure.

Portals

Three people, drawn from our world and forced into new bodies, face dark forces in a shattered land of demons, undead, and magic. Can they overcome their own demons and save two worlds?

Journal of a Stranger

Time traveler Jack Tucker shares his thoughts, ideas, philosophies, and inspirations and experiences across 70,000 years of the past, present, and future in the form of his private diary..

The Downfall

The magical emanations of the comet, the Talisman, brought insectile horrors from the bowels of the earth, increased the powers of an insane necromancer and a shape-shifting, demon-summoning race. Can five people forced together by fate survive knowing the world is ending, and still fight to save it?

Travis I. Sivart